TOP 10 BASEBALL HOME RUN HITTERS

Bill Deane

SPORTS TOP 10

 Enslow Publishers, Inc.

44 Fadem Road	PO Box 38
Box 699	Aldershot
Springfield, NJ 07081	Hants GU12 6BP
USA	UK

DEDICATION

To Sarah, one of the Top 10 Daughters of all time.

ACKNOWLEDGMENTS

The author wishes to thank Bryan Reilly (PF Sports Images) and Mark Rucker (Transcendental Graphics), for their help in providing the photographs for this book; Scot Mondore, Bruce Markusen, and Dan Bennett of the National Baseball Library & Archive, for their research assistance; and, especially, Sarah Deane, for her expert help in reading the manuscript for this book from a young person's viewpoint.

Library of Congress Cataloging-in-Publication Data

Deane, Bill.
    Top 10 baseball home run hitters / Bill Deane.
      p. cm. — (Sports top 10)
    Includes bibliographical references and index.
    Summary: Presents profiles of ten players, including Hank Aaron, Harmon Killebrew, Jimmie Foxx, Mickey Mantle, William McCovey, Fred McGriff, Babe Ruth, Mike Schmidt, Roger Maris, and Frank Thomas, whose home run percentages and "slugging percentages" were among the highest in baseball's history.
    ISBN 0-89490-804-9
      1. Baseball players—United States—Biography—Juvenile literature.
2. Baseball players—Rating of—United States—Juvenile literature. 3. Batting (Baseball)—Juvenile literature. [1. Baseball players. 2. Home runs (Baseball)] I. Title. II. Title: Top 10 baseball home run hitters. III. Series.
GV865.A1D373 1997
796.357'092'2
[B]—dc20   96-39057
                                  CIP
                                  AC

Illustration Credits: AP/Wide World Photos, p. 35; PF Sports Images, Yonkers, NY, pp. 7, 15, 17, 23, 25, 27, 29, 30, 33, 41, 43, 45; Transcendental Graphics, Boulder, Colo., pp. 9, 10, 13, 18, 21, 37, 39.

Cover Credit: PF Sports Images, Yonkers, NY.

Interior Design: Richard Stalzer.

CONTENTS

INTRODUCTION

WHAT MAKES A GREAT HOME RUN hitter? Is it sheer strength? A huge bat?

Home run champions and their weapons have come in all shapes and sizes. Frank Howard, who twice led the American League in homers, was six feet seven inches tall and weighed 260 pounds. But Jumbo Brown, at six feet four inches and 295 pounds, failed to hit a homer in 157 big league times at bat. Mel Ott, who topped the National League six times, stood just five feet nine inches and weighed 170 pounds. Twelve-time home run champ Babe Ruth used a bat weighing forty-seven ounces. Ed Roush used a fifty-ounce stick, but never hit more than eight homers in a season. And Hank Aaron, the man who broke Ruth's career home run record, used a bat weighing just thirty-two ounces. Obviously, there is no special formula for a home run hitter. It usually is a special player with sharp eyes, a strong body, quick wrists, and split-second timing.

This book profiles our choices for the ten best home run hitters in baseball history. In selecting them, we looked at such things as total number of home runs and league leaderships. We also paid particular attention to an unusual statistic called "home run percentage" (HR%): the average number of homers a player hits per one hundred times at bat. Another important statistic is "slugging percentage," the average number of total bases made by a hitter per time at bat. If a player can maintain a HR% of six or higher, and a slugging percentage of .500 or better, he will rank among the very best sluggers in the game.

In narrowing the list down to ten, we had to leave out many great home run hitters. These include Willie Mays, Ralph Kiner, Ted Williams, Lou Gehrig, Frank Robinson, Reggie Jackson, Ed Mathews, Dave Kingman, Willie

Stargell, Mark McGwire, Albert Belle, Ken Griffey, Jr., and Negro Leagues' star Josh Gibson. Some of these men hit a lot of homers, but were better known for their all-around play and didn't rank so high in HR%. Others did well in HR%, but didn't play long or consistently enough to make higher career totals.

But, we won't apologize for the ten selections we did make. These are the players who create excitement in the fans and fear in the pitchers, with the knowledge that one swing of their bat can send a baseball into orbit and break open a ballgame. Their statistics are summarized below:

CAREER STATISTICS

Player	YR	G	R	H	HR	HR%	HIGH	LL	RBI	AVG	SLG
HANK AARON	23	3298	2174	3771	755	6.11	47	4	2297	.305	.555
JIMMIE FOXX	20	2317	1751	2646	534	6.57	58	4	1921	.325	.609
HARMON KILLEBREW	22	2435	1283	2086	573	7.03	49	6	1584	.256	.509
MICKEY MANTLE	18	2401	1677	2415	536	6.62	54	4	1509	.298	.557
ROGER MARIS	12	1463	826	1325	275	5.39	61	1	850	.260	.476
WILLIE MCCOVEY	22	2588	1229	2211	521	6.36	45	3	1555	.270	.515
FRED MCGRIFF	11	1450	869	1466	317	6.18	37	2	910	.286	.530
BABE RUTH	22	2503	2174	2873	714	8.50	60	12	2211	.342	.690
MIKE SCHMIDT	18	2404	1506	2234	548	6.56	48	8	1595	.267	.527
FRANK THOMAS	7	930	675	1077	222	6.75	41	0	729	.327	.599

KEY:
YR = years in majors
G = games played
R = runs scored
H = hits
HR = home runs

HR% = home run percentage
HIGH = highest single-season home run total
LL = league home run leaderships
RBI = runs batted in
AVG = batting average
SLG = slugging percentage

HANK AARON

BABE RUTH'S RECORD OF 714 career home runs had stood since 1935, and people thought it would last forever. But, after twenty years of excellence, the Braves' Hank Aaron needed only one homer to shatter this "unbreakable" record. Millions of TV viewers tuned in on April 8, 1974, to see whether Aaron could do it.

Aaron had more on his mind than the record, however. As he approached it, he was hounded by reporters wherever he went. More disturbing, he received thousands of letters—much of it racist hate mail, even death threats. It was from people who didn't want the African-American Aaron to break the white Ruth's record. Hank blocked it all out, ending the drama on his first swing. In the fourth inning, he drilled a pitch into the left-center-field bullpen, his 715th lifetime homer. "Thank God it's over," Aaron said.[1]

Henry Louis Aaron was born in Mobile, Alabama, on February 5, 1934. There, he attended Central High School before graduating from Josephine Allen Institute. Although neither school had a baseball team, Henry had become an outstanding baseball and softball player in local leagues. He joined the Indianapolis Clowns, a Negro League team, before being noticed by Braves' scouts. Henry then signed with their organization, and batted .353 in the minor leagues.

Aaron broke into the majors when he was twenty. Though not a large man, the right-handed batter impressed observers with his muscular forearms and quick wrists. Because of this, he could wait longer than most hitters

Keeping his eye on the ball, Hank Aaron looks to hammer the incoming pitch into the seats. During his career, Aaron led the league in home runs four times.

before deciding whether to swing. He sometimes seemed to hit the ball right out of the catcher's glove!

Aaron soon became one of the most complete players in the game. In 1956, he won the National League batting title and Player of the Year Award. A year later, he led the Braves to the world championship with 44 home runs—including the one that clinched the pennant—and was named the league's MVP. Over his first twelve seasons, he batted .320, won three Gold Glove awards for excellence in the outfield, and became one of the league's top base-stealers. Hammerin' Hank hit line drives to all fields, and the home run was only one weapon in his arsenal. But, because he wasn't talkative or flashy, or didn't play in a media center like New York, Aaron's performances went almost unnoticed.

All those years, the Braves played in Milwaukee's County Stadium, a difficult place to hit home runs. But in 1966, the team moved to Atlanta, where balls seemed to jump out of the park. Aaron decided he could now help the team more by trying to hit homers. He led the National League in 1966 and 1967, and hit his 500th homer a year later.

It was about this time that people started to realize that Hank had a chance at Ruth's record. Aaron didn't let them down: from age thirty five to thirty nine, when most players are winding down, he averaged 41 home runs a year. Hank finally retired in 1976 with 755 homers in all, one of many records he still holds.

Most baseball fans know that Hank holds the home run record, but few remember what a great all-around player he was. As longtime big league player and broadcaster Bob Uecker said, Aaron was "the most underrated player of my time, and his."[2]

HANK AARON

BORN: February 5, 1934, Mobile, Alabama.

HIGH SCHOOL: Central High School and Josephine Allen Institute, Mobile, Alabama.

PRO: Milwaukee Braves, 1954–1965; Atlanta Braves, 1966–1974; Milwaukee Brewers, 1975–1976.

RECORDS: Most home runs, 755; Most runs batted in, 2,297; Most extra-base hits, 1,477; Most total bases on hits, 6,856.

HONORS: NL MVP, 1957; NL Player of the Year, 1956, 1963; Gold Glove, 1958–1960; Elected to National Baseball Hall of Fame, 1982.

In 1954, Hank Aaron joined the Milwaukee Braves as a twenty-year-old rookie. He led the Braves to a World Series victory in 1957, which was only his fourth season.

JIMMIE FOXX

Getting ready for his next at bat, Jimmie Foxx takes some practice swings in the on-deck circle. All of his practicing certainly paid off in 1933 when Foxx won the American League Triple Crown.

AFTER WINNING THE FIRST TWO games of the 1930 World Series, the Philadelphia Athletics seemed to go to sleep. They lost the next two games against the Cardinals and scored only one run in a span of thirty innings. The winner of game five would be one victory away from the World Championship.

Neither team scored in the first eight innings. In the ninth, it came down to a battle of two future Hall of Famers: the Cardinals' crafty thirty-seven-year-old pitcher, Burleigh Grimes, against the A's strong twenty-two-year-old slugger, Jimmie Foxx. Grimes came in with a curveball and Foxx took a mighty swing. The ball soared high and deep, finally landing in the left-center-field bleachers to win the game for the A's. Foxx called it "the biggest homer I ever hit."[1]

James Emory Foxx was born in Sudlersville, Maryland, on October 22, 1907. Jimmie built powerful muscles working on the family farm, and was the size of an adult by the time he was thirteen. He starred in local baseball games, showing a strong throwing arm and blazing speed in addition to his batting power. He left Sudlersville High School to become a professional ballplayer when he was sixteen.

Within a year, Jimmie was in the major leagues. Manager Connie Mack worked him into the lineup little by little, before giving him a regular job at age twenty-one. Foxx played catcher, third base, and outfield—he eventually played every position except second base—before finally finding his home at first base. In Jimmie's first year as a full-time player, he had 33 homers and a .354 average to help the Athletics to the 1929 world championship.

Foxx led the A's to championships in the next two years as well, batting a combined .344 in the three World Series. Then, he truly arrived as a slugger. In 1932, Foxx hit an amazing 58 home runs, driving in 169 runs and batting .364. He became the first American Leaguer to out-homer Babe Ruth since 1925, and he nearly broke Ruth's single-season home run record of 60 in the process.

Foxx followed with another awesome season, winning the Triple Crown and his second straight MVP with 48 homers, 163 RBIs, and a .356 average. He had become known as "The Beast" for his huge muscles and monstrous home runs. Jimmie was in the midst of twelve straight seasons with 30 or more homers, a major league record.

Traded to the Red Sox in 1935, Foxx kept on slugging. In 1938, he became the first man to win three MVP Awards, after a season of 50 homers, 175 RBIs, and a .349 average. Two years later, at age thirty-two, he became the youngest man ever to reach 500 career homers.

Physical problems were beginning to wear down Foxx's body, however. He suffered from a chronic sinus problem that affected his vision, and battled tonsillitis, appendicitis, cracked ribs, broken fingers, and torn knee cartilage at various times. It was all compounded by a drinking problem. Foxx was washed up by his mid-thirties.

Nevertheless, he finished with 534 homers, which for two decades ranked second behind only Ruth. As noted writer Joe Williams said, Foxx was "the most powerful right-hand slugger baseball ever knew."[2]

JIMMIE FOXX

BORN: October 22, 1907, Sudlersville, Maryland.

DIED: July 21, 1967, Miami, Florida.

HIGH SCHOOL: Sudlersville High School, Sudlersville, Maryland (did not graduate).

PRO: Philadelphia Athletics, 1925–1935; Boston Red Sox, 1936–1942; Chicago Cubs, 1942, 1944; Philadelphia Phillies, 1945.

RECORDS: Most consecutive years (12) with 30 or more home runs (1929–1940).

HONORS: AL MVP, 1932, 1933, 1938; Elected to National Baseball Hall of Fame, 1951.

Jimmie Foxx holds a major league record for hitting 30 or more home runs in twelve consecutive seasons. Foxx was elected to the National Baseball Hall of Fame in 1951.

HARMON KILLEBREW

HARMON KILLEBREW'S CAREER WAS IN jeopardy. During the 1968 All-Star Game, the thirty-two-year-old Twins' slugger had suffered a badly-ruptured hamstring muscle. "It was as severe an injury as I've seen," said the team doctor. "We thought this could be the end of his career and so did he."[1]

Killebrew refused to give up. He spent the winter walking, stretching, and lifting weights to strengthen his leg. He wound up playing all 162 games in 1969 and won the American League's MVP Award.

Harmon Clayton Killebrew was born in Payette, Idaho, on June 29, 1936. He starred in baseball, football, and basketball at Payette High School, and briefly attended the College of Idaho. A family friend recommended young Harmon to the owner of the Washington Senators. A Senators' scout watched Killebrew hit a 435-foot homer in a local game, and promptly signed him up. Harmon played in his first big league game before his eighteenth birthday.

Killebrew was not an instant success, however. Between 1954 and 1958, he mostly sat on the bench and shuffled between the major and minor leagues. Harmon started his career as a second baseman, and later played regularly at third base, first base, and the outfield. He willingly played wherever the team needed him, and he became the first man to start All-Star Games at each of three different positions.

The Senators finally gave him a full-time job in 1959, and Harmon responded by hitting 42 home runs to tie for the league lead. Two years later, the Senators moved to Minnesota to become the Twins, and Killebrew started a

Throughout his career, Killebrew was named to thirteen All-Star teams. He was inducted into the National Baseball Hall of Fame in 1984.

streak of four straight seasons with 45 or more homers in each, something only Babe Ruth had done. After hitting 46 in 1961, Harmon led the American League with 48, 45, and 49 in the next three seasons. Killebrew helped the Twins to the World Series in 1965, and had big seasons in 1966 and 1967.

Killebrew was stocky, with big biceps and a thick neck. His swing brought fear to opposing teams, who nicknamed him "Killer." Extending his muscular wrists and swiveling his hips, Killebrew hit long home runs, many estimated at more than five hundred feet.

Rebounding from his hamstring injury, Killebrew led the American League with 49 homers, 140 RBIs, 145 walks, and a .430 on-base average in 1969. A year later, he led the Twins to a second straight divisional title with 41 homers. He was named American League Player of the Year in both seasons. Despite numerous injuries, Killebrew averaged 40 homers and 103 RBIs per year between 1959 and 1970.

Although Killebrew was a slow runner and below-average fielder, and didn't hit for a high batting average (.256 lifetime), experts recognized his true value. He was named to thirteen All-Star teams, finished in the top five in MVP voting six times, and was elected to the Hall of Fame in 1984.

All in all, Killebrew hit 573 home runs, fifth on the all-time list, and more than any other right-handed hitter in American League history. His home run percentage of 7.03 ranks fourth-highest ever. He topped 40 homers in eight seasons, leading the league six times. As award-winning sportswriter Dick Young said, "Harmon Killebrew is the purest home run hitter, next to Babe Ruth, ever to put on a uniform."[2]

HARMON KILLEBREW

BORN: June 29, 1936, Payette, Idaho.

HIGH SCHOOL: Payette High School, Payette, Idaho.

COLLEGE: College of Idaho, Caldwell, Idaho (did not graduate).

PRO: Washington Senators, 1954–1960; Minnesota Twins, 1961–1974; Kansas City Royals, 1975.

RECORDS: Most career home runs, right-handed batter, AL, 573.

HONORS: AL MVP, 1969; AL Player of the Year, 1969, 1970; Elected to National Baseball Hall of Fame, 1984.

Harmon Killebrew ranks fifth on the all-time home run list with 573. He either led the league or tied for the league lead in home runs six times.

MICKEY MANTLE

One of the most popular baseball players ever, Mickey Mantle was known for hitting home runs in important games. Mantle holds the major-league record for most home runs in World Series play.

MICKEY MANTLE

GAME THREE OF THE 1964 World Series was tied going into the bottom of the ninth inning. The winner of this game would take a 2-1 lead in the Series. The Cardinals brought in their ace relief pitcher to face Yankees' slugger Mickey Mantle. Mantle, at age thirty-two, was already playing in his twelfth Fall Classic. He had hit 15 Series home runs, tied with Babe Ruth for the most ever.

Mantle swung at the first pitch and sent the ball deep into the right field stands. With one flick of the bat, the Yankees had won, 2–1, and Mickey Mantle had become the most productive home run hitter in World Series history. Mantle called it "the biggest thrill I ever had."[1]

Mickey Charles Mantle—named after Hall of Fame catcher Mickey Cochrane—was born in Spavinaw, Oklahoma, on October 20, 1931. He grew up in nearby Commerce, where his father spent hour after hour teaching Mickey how to play ball, and how to switch-hit. Mickey turned pro the day he graduated from Commerce High School.

Within two years, Mantle was a nineteen-year-old rookie with the Yankees. He could run like the wind (he was timed at 3.1 seconds running from home to first base) and hit with astonishing power from either side of the plate. Mickey struggled at first, but then started living up to expectations. On April 17, 1953, the young center fielder amazed the baseball world by hitting a home run measured at 565 feet. "No doubt about it," said Clark Griffith, who had been in pro ball as a player, manager, and executive since 1888. "That was the longest home run ever hit in the history of baseball."[2]

Mantle won his first home run title in 1955, but he really came of age in 1956: he led the American League with 52 home runs, 130 RBIs, and a .353 batting average to unanimously win the MVP Award. Mantle was challenging to win another Triple Crown the following year before an injury stopped him with 34 homers and a .365 average—good enough for his second straight MVP.

Mickey continued to excel, winning homer crowns in 1958 and 1960, hitting a career-high 54 circuit clouts in 1961, and earning his third MVP Award in 1962. But, a long history of injuries began to take its toll. Mantle missed an average of fifty games per year between 1962–66. When he did play, he had both legs taped from ankle to thigh before each game, and was in constant agony. "Mickey has a greater capacity to withstand pain than any man I've ever seen," said longtime Yankees' trainer Joe Soares.[3]

Mickey was forced to retire at age thirty-six, but not before he reached some milestones. In 1964, he extended his World Series home run record to 18. In 1967, he became only the sixth player to reach 500 homers. In 1968, he passed Ted Williams and Jimmie Foxx to finish his career third on the all-time home run list.

Mantle was elected to the Hall of Fame in his first try in 1974. In spite of his achievements, most observers preferred to imagine what Mickey *might* have accomplished, if not for his physical problems. "Mantle 100 percent physically sound through his career," said one writer, "would have been the greatest player who ever lived."[4]

MICKEY MANTLE

BORN: October 20, 1931, Spavinaw, Oklahoma.

DIED: August 13, 1995, Dallas, Texas.

HIGH SCHOOL: Commerce High School, Commerce, Oklahoma.

PRO: New York Yankees, 1951–1968.

RECORDS: Most times, home runs from both sides of plate, game, AL, 10; most home runs, switch-hitter, 536; most World Series home runs, 18, RBIs, 40, and runs, 42.

HONORS: Triple Crown, 1956; AL MVP, 1956, 1957, 1962; AL Player of the Year, 1956, 1962; Gold Glove, 1962; Elected to National Baseball Hall of Fame, 1974.

Putting all of his strength into it, Mickey Mantle swings for the fences. Mantle eventually won three Most Valuable Player awards, and finished his career with 536 home runs.

ROGER MARIS

BABE RUTH'S RECORD OF 60 home runs in one season had stood for thirty-four years. But late in 1961, the Yankees' Roger Maris tied it. Maris entered the season's last game needing one homer to break the record.

In the fourth inning, Maris ripped into a fastball and sent it into the right-field seats. The homer not only set a new record, but won the game, 1–0. "It gives me a wonderful feeling to know that I'm the only man in history to hit 61 home runs," said Maris afterward. "Nobody can take that away from me."[1]

Roger Eugene Maras (later changed to Maris) was born in Hibbing, Minnesota, September 10, 1934. Roger grew up in North Dakota, where he attended Fargo Central and Bishop Shanley High Schools. Shanley had no baseball team, but Roger starred in Little League and American Legion baseball as a youth.

Maris began his pro career at age eighteen in 1953. After a four-year climb through the minor leagues, Roger made it to the majors with the Cleveland Indians. A year later, he joined the Kansas City Athletics. Maris hit just .249 in his first three seasons, with an average of only 19 homers per season.

But the Yankees liked what they saw in Maris: an excellent outfielder with a strong left-handed swing. It was perfect for Yankee Stadium's short right-field fence. In December 1959, New York traded four men to get Roger and two other players. It became one of the best deals the team ever made. In 1960, Maris hit 39 homers, topped the American League in RBIs and slugging, and won the Gold

ROGER MARIS

In 1961, Maris was awarded his second consecutive MVP award. Only five other players have won consecutive AL MVP awards. They are Jimmie Foxx, Hal Newhouser, Yogi Berra, Mickey Mantle, and Frank Thomas.

Glove award for fielding. He led the Yankees to the first of five straight pennants, and was named the league's Most Valuable Player.

After a slow start in 1961, Maris began hitting homers in bunches. He and teammate Mickey Mantle were not only battling for the home run title, but threatening Ruth's famous record. By the end of July, Maris already had 40 homers; Mantle had hit 39. Health problems forced Mantle out of the race in mid-September, and Maris was left to challenge the Babe alone. Despite tremendous media pressure, Roger succeeded, hitting that 61st home run on October 1. In addition, he tied for the league leads with 132 runs scored and 141 RBIs. The Yankees went on to win the World Series, and Maris earned numerous honors, including his second straight MVP Award.

But, it wasn't enough to please everyone. Fans and writers criticized him in comparison to Ruth and Mantle. They wanted Roger to hit 62 homers to prove 1961 was more than luck. Although Maris led the Yankees to another world championship with 33 homers and 100 RBIs in 1962, people were not impressed. "If a vote were taken," said one sportswriter, "Roger Maris undoubtedly would be elected flop of the year."[2]

Maris became a bitter man who no longer enjoyed playing baseball. To make it worse, he suffered through a series of injuries starting in 1963. He was finally traded to the St. Louis Cardinals. After helping them to two straight World Series, Maris retired at age thirty-four.

Maris preferred to be remembered as simply a good all-around player, which is what he was for most of his twelve-year career. But, for one season, Maris was the greatest home run hitter in baseball history, and his record has now lasted longer than Ruth's did.

ROGER MARIS

BORN: September 10, 1934, Hibbing, Minnesota.

DIED: December 14, 1985, Houston, Texas.

HIGH SCHOOL: Fargo Central and Bishop Shanley Catholic High
School, Fargo, North Dakota.

PRO: Cleveland Indians, 1957–1958; Kansas City Athletics,
1958–1959; New York Yankees, 1960–1966; St. Louis
Cardinals, 1967–1968.

RECORDS: Most home runs, season (61 in 1961).

HONORS: AL MVP, 1960–1961; AL Player of the Year, 1961; Gold
Glove, 1960.

In 1961, Roger Maris broke Babe Ruth's record by hitting 61 home
runs. Since then, the most home runs hit in one season has been 52,
accomplished by Willie Mays (1965), George Foster (1977), and
Mark McGwire (1996).

Willie McCovey

The Experts Figured Willie McCovey was through. Once a champion slugger, Willie now was thirty-nine years old with a long history of physical problems. McCovey had batted a poor .203 with just seven home runs in 1976. He had been released by two teams, and no other club seemed to want him.

But Willie was sure that the experts were wrong. He asked his old team, the San Francisco Giants, to give him a try-out the following spring. The Giants took a chance on McCovey and he rewarded their faith by leading the team in home runs and RBIs, and earning the "Comeback Player of the Year" award. Willie finally retired three years later, having hit 521 home runs—more than any other left-handed hitter in National League history.

Willie Lee McCovey was born January 10, 1938, in Mobile, Alabama, the same city that had produced Hank Aaron. Willie became a three-sport star at Central High School, but his first love was baseball. He left school to turn pro at seventeen, and began an impressive climb up the minor league ladder.

The six-foot-four-inch first baseman joined the Giants on July 30, 1959. Willie had a relaxed-looking stance, but when he got his pitch, he would explode with a looping upper-cut swing that usually sent the ball screaming toward right field. McCovey slammed four hits in his first big league game, and went on to bat a whopping .354 with 13 homers in just 52 games. He was chosen as Rookie of the Year.

But the Giants already had an All-Star first baseman, Orlando Cepeda. Over the next three years, McCovey

WILLIE McCOVEY

Willie McCovey's best season was in 1969, when he won the NL MVP award. He finished his career with 521 home runs, and was elected to the National Baseball Hall of Fame in 1986.

served only as a part-time player. Finally, Willie was given a chance to play regularly in 1963, and he responded by hitting 44 home runs to tie Aaron for the league lead. Strangely enough, both players wore number 44.

Starting in 1965, McCovey had more than 30 homers in each of six straight seasons, becoming the most respected slugger in the game. In both 1968 and 1969, he led the National League in home runs, RBIs, and slugging percentage. He won the 1969 MVP Award by batting .320 with 45 homers and 126 RBIs. Opposing teams were so afraid of Willie, he was intentionally walked a major-league record 45 times that year—sometimes even with the bases empty!

McCovey had another big year in 1970, with 39 homers, 126 RBIs, 40 intentional walks, and his third straight slugging title. Then injuries, including a broken arm, arthritic knees, and bone chips in his hips, began to take their toll. Willie missed more than three hundred games over the next six years, until his dramatic comeback. He played until age forty-two, setting National League records for most career grand slams (18), and most homers by a first baseman. McCovey was elected to the Hall of Fame in 1986, his very first try.

McCovey's career touched four decades, from a spectacular debut in the 1950s to a Hall of Fame finish in the 1980s. It takes more than talent to last and produce for that long. "You've got to have that drive," said McCovey. "Things like that are what separate the superstars from the good ballplayers."[1]

WILLIE McCOVEY

BORN: January 10, 1938, Mobile, Alabama.

HIGH SCHOOL: Central High School, Mobile, Alabama.

PRO: San Francisco Giants, 1959–1973, 1977–1980; San Diego Padres, 1974–1976; Oakland A's, 1976.

RECORDS: Most intentional walks, season, 45 (1969); Most grand slams, NL, 18; Most home runs, left-handed hitter, NL, 521; Most home runs, first baseman, NL, 439.

HONORS: NL Rookie of the Year, 1959; NL MVP, 1969; Major League Player of the Year, 1969; Elected to National Baseball Hall of Fame, 1986.

Knowing that he hit the ball well, Willie McCovey watches it sail out of the yard. In his first season, McCovey batted .354 and won the Rookie of the Year award.

FRED McGRIFF

Using his fluid swing, Fred McGriff launches another homer. McGriff won the 1994 All-Star Game MVP Award, by hitting a game-tying home run in the ninth inning.

FRED McGRIFF

IT LOOKED AS IF THE National League was going to lose its seventh All-Star Game in a row. In the bottom of the ninth inning of the 1994 contest, the American League held a 7–5 lead, with all-time saves leader Lee Smith to protect it.

But the National League still had a secret weapon on the bench. With one out and a man on base, they sent Atlanta Braves' slugger Fred McGriff up to pinch-hit. McGriff drilled a ball over the left-center field fence, and suddenly it was all tied up. The National League went on to win, 8–7, and McGriff was named the game's MVP. "It's the stuff you dream about," said McGriff.[1]

Frederick Stanley McGriff was born in Tampa, Florida, on October 31, 1963, and attended Jefferson High School there. "I was always around a baseball atmosphere," Fred explains. "With the weather down in Tampa, you can almost play year around and that's all I wanted to do."[2] McGriff turned down a college scholarship, and signed with the Yankees to begin his pro baseball career at seventeen.

Fred was traded to the Toronto Blue Jays' organization in 1982. He went to spring training with the Jays for four years in a row before finally making the cut in 1987, and earned a regular spot a year later. McGriff responded by finishing second in the league in both home runs and slugging percentage. In 1989, his 36 homers topped the American League and led Toronto to the League Championship Series.

A year later, Fred was traded to the San Diego Padres in a blockbuster deal that sent Roberto Alomar and Joe Carter to Toronto. McGriff had two more solid years and, in 1992, led the National League with 35 homers. The big first baseman thus became the first player since 1908 to win home run titles in both leagues.

In the middle of the 1993 season, McGriff was traded to Atlanta. Fred fired up the team's offense and led the Braves to the National League Championship Series, where he hit .435 in a losing cause. McGriff had his best all-around season in the strike-shortened 1994 campaign, batting .318 with 34 homers in just 113 games. It was his seventh consecutive season with 30 or more home runs, a feat accomplished previously by only eight players, all Hall of Famers.

The strike shortened the 1995 season as well, costing McGriff a chance at another 30-homer season. Nevertheless, Fred powered the Braves to the top of the baseball world. He led the team in homers and RBIs, then batted .333 with 4 home runs in 14 post-season games as Atlanta won its first world championship. He was rewarded with a four-year, $20 million contract.

McGriff is not a typical slugger. The soft-spoken family man uses a wispy thirty-two-and-one-half-ounce bat, and has a swing which looks more like a tennis return than a power-punch. The lefty hits to all fields and tries just to hit the ball hard, not necessarily over the fence.

McGriff's home run totals from 1988 through 1996 are a study in consistency: 34, 36, 35, 31, 35, 37, 34, 27, 28. McGriff is quietly proud of his reliability. When asked how he would want to be remembered, he says, "that I was consistent . . . as a guy who went out every day and gave 100 percent."[3]

FRED McGRIFF

BORN: October 31, 1963, Tampa, Florida.

HIGH SCHOOL: Jefferson High School, Tampa, Florida.

PRO: Toronto Blue Jays, 1986–1990; San Diego Padres, 1991–1993; Atlanta Braves, 1993– .

Fred McGriff consistently gives all that he has to offer on the baseball field. From 1988 to 1994, McGriff hit over 30 home runs each year.

BABE RUTH

BABE RUTH WAS GETTING OLD, and fans and players in enemy ballparks wouldn't let him forget it. At thirty-seven, Ruth was slower and heavier than in his glory days as the "Sultan of Swat." As his Yankees arrived in Chicago for Game Three of the 1932 World Series, the Cubs and their audience were really on Ruth's case.

Ruth came to bat in the fifth inning and, with two strikes, gestured out toward the field. Many observers thought the Babe was "calling his shot," indicating that he would hit a home run. Ruth then hit the next pitch far over the right-center-field fence, giving the Yankees the lead for good. Babe Ruth was still the Sultan of Swat!

George Herman Ruth was born in Baltimore, Maryland, on February 6, 1895. A problem child, he spent age seven through nineteen at a Catholic reform school. It was there that Ruth developed his baseball skills, and where he was discovered by Jack Dunn, owner of Baltimore's minor league team. Dunn had to become Ruth's legal guardian in order to take him from the school, and people began referring to the youngster as "Dunn's Babe."

An outstanding pitcher, the Babe quickly made it to the major leagues. He pitched for the Red Sox for six years, becoming the best left-hander in the league. But, he was also an excellent hitter, and some thought he could win more games for Boston batting every day instead of pitching every fourth day. The Red Sox eventually converted Ruth into a full-time outfielder.

Before this time, home runs were scarce. Teams played for one run at a time, hitters choked up on the bat, and balls

BABE RUTH

Many people argue that Babe Ruth was the best hitter of all time. Besides hitting 714 home runs, Ruth also is second all-time in runs batted in, and tenth all-time in batting average.

were left in play until they were soft and gray. It usually took only about ten home runs to lead the league. But in 1919, Ruth astonished everyone, taking big swings with a huge bat, and hitting 29 homers, a new major league record.

The Babe was only warming up. Sold to New York in 1920, Ruth almost doubled his own record by belting 54 homers. A year later, he hit 59. In just three seasons, he had hit more home runs than anyone else had hit in an entire career! Because of Ruth's success and popularity, other players began aiming for the fences, and the game was changed forever.

Ruth's slugging turned the Yankees from a mediocre team to a champion, and doubled their attendance. In 1923, Babe batted .393, won the MVP Award, and led the Yanks to their first world championship. Ruth would play in ten World Series during his career, hitting 15 homers.

Ruth's habits of eating and drinking too much caught up with him in 1925. Many thought he was washed up. But, the Babe came back strong, and averaged 50 homers per year over the next six seasons. He peaked at 60 in 1927, which was more than any other American League team that year!

On May 25, 1935, Ruth hit three long home runs to give him a career total of 714—more than double anybody else's total to that point. He retired five days later, the best-known and most-loved sports figure of all time. His lifetime home run percentage (8.50) and slugging percentage (.690) are by far the best ever. As one writer asked, "what further laurels may we add to the man who already towers head and shoulders above all other sluggers of this or any other time?"[1]

BABE RUTH

BORN: February 6, 1895, Baltimore, Maryland.

DIED: August 16, 1948, New York, New York.

HIGH SCHOOL: St. Mary's Industrial School for Boys, Baltimore, Maryland.

PRO: Boston Red Sox, 1914–1919; New York Yankees, 1920–1934; Boston Braves, 1935.

RECORDS: Most home runs by left-handed batter, 714; Most home runs, AL, 708; Most home runs, outfielder, 692; Most years leading league in home runs, 12; Most runs scored, season (177 in 1921); Most bases on balls, season (170 in 1923) and career (2,056); Highest slugging percentage, season (.847 in 1920) and career (.690); Highest home run percentage and career (8.50).

HONORS: AL MVP, 1923; Elected to National Baseball Hall of Fame, 1936.

During the 1932 World Series, Babe Ruth pointed to a place in the right-field bleachers, and then promptly hit a home run into that part of the ballpark. Shown here is a photo of that historic moment.

AFTER NINETY-SEVEN YEARS IN THE league, the Phillies still had never won a World Series. In three of the past four years, the team had won the Eastern Division title, only to lose in the League Championship Series. Some people blamed the team's best player, Mike Schmidt. They said he "choked," or failed in important situations.

That all changed in 1980. The Phillies and Expos were tied for first place, and would finish the season with three games against each other. In the first game, Schmidt drove in both runs in a 2–1 Phillies' victory. In the second, Mike's homer in the eleventh inning won the game, 6–4, and gave Philadelphia the divisional title. The Phillies then won the LCS and advanced to the World Series. In six games there, Schmidt batted .381, hit two homers, and drove in seven runs, including the two that won the final game. The Phillies were World Champions, and Schmidt was the Series MVP. "This has to be the highest point of my athletic career," said Schmidt.[1]

Michael Jack Schmidt was born in Dayton, Ohio, on September 27, 1949. He was a Little League star in Dayton, and graduated from Fairview High School. Mike then attended Ohio University, where he became an All-American shortstop. He had excellent hand-eye coordination, which contributed toward his fine hitting and fielding abilities. The Phillies made him a second-round draft choice in 1971.

Schmidt became the Phillies' regular third baseman by 1973, but he struggled at first and batted only .196 as a rookie. He worked hard to improve, and it paid off. In 1974,

In 1980, Mike Schmidt's spectacular play earned him the World Series Most Valuable Player Award, as the Phillies beat the Kansas City Royals for the championship.

MIKE SCHMIDT

he batted .282, led the National League in home runs and slugging, and set a league fielding record for most assists in one season.

Schmidt also topped the league in homers the next two seasons. In 1976, he tied a record with four consecutive homers in one game. He also won his first of ten Gold Gloves for fielding excellence, and led the Phillies to their first of three straight divisional titles.

In 1979, all-time great Pete Rose joined the Phillies. Rose convinced Schmidt he had the talent to become the best player in the game. Schmidt proceeded to hit 45 homers that year and 48 in 1980, the Phillies' World Championship year. Schmidt led the league in homers, RBIs, and slugging (.624), and was unanimously named the league's MVP.

Schmidt had his best year in the strike-shortened 1981 season. He batted a career-high .316 and led the league in runs, homers, RBIs, walks, on-base percentage, and slugging (.644), earning his second straight MVP. Despite injuries, he continued to have one outstanding year after another. In 1986, he won his third MVP and set a record by leading the National League in home runs for the eighth time.

Schmidt retired in 1989 with several fielding records and 548 career home runs, setting the record for most homers by a third baseman. He was named "Player of the Decade" for the 1980s, and was elected to the Hall of Fame in his first try, receiving 97 percent of the possible votes. Experts are impressed by the combination of Schmidt's destructive hitting and his excellent fielding at an important position. As one writer summarized, "analysts say Schmidt is the best all-around third baseman—and one of the top dozen players—in the annals of the game."[2]

MIKE SCHMIDT

BORN: September 27, 1949, Dayton, Ohio.

HIGH SCHOOL: Fairview High School, Dayton, Ohio.

COLLEGE: Ohio University, Athens, Ohio.

PRO: Philadelphia Phillies, 1972–1989.

RECORDS: Most home runs, game, 4 (April 17, 1976); Most home runs, third baseman, season (48 in 1980) and career (509); most times leading NL in home runs, 8.

HONORS: NL MVP, 1980, 1981, 1986; NL Player of the Year, 1980, 1986; Major League Player of the Decade, 1990; Gold Glove, 1976–1984, 1986; Elected to National Baseball Hall of Fame, 1995.

Throughout his eighteen-year career, Mike Schmidt was always a home run threat. He holds the NL record for most times leading the league in homers with 8.

FRANK THOMAS

WINNING A MVP AWARD CAN sometimes be a curse. Many players seem to get a little self-satisfied, while the opposing players try extra hard to beat them. In the history of the MVP Award, only ten out of 146 winners had managed to win again the next year. This was what Frank Thomas, the 1993 American League MVP, was up against.

But Thomas was even better in 1994. In the strike-shortened season, he batted .353 and cracked 38 homers in 113 games. His .729 slugging percentage and .487 on-base percentage were among the best of all time. He was overwhelmingly named MVP again.

Frank Edward Thomas, Jr., was born May 27, 1968, in Columbus, Georgia. Frank attended Columbus High School and starred in three sports. Although baseball was his favorite, scouts considered the huge muscleman more of a football player, ignoring him in baseball's 1986 Free Agent draft. Disappointed, Thomas accepted a football scholarship to Auburn University.

A leg injury a year later ended Frank's football career, enabling him to devote his full attention to baseball. He was an all-Southeastern Conference selection in each of his three years at Auburn, and set a school record with 49 career home runs. In 1989, the Chicago White Sox made him the nation's seventh player selected in the Free Agent draft.

The six-foot-five-inch, 257-pound first baseman earned the call to the big leagues barely a year later, and made his debut with the White Sox on August 2, 1990. Over the last two months of the season he blasted the ball at a .330 clip,

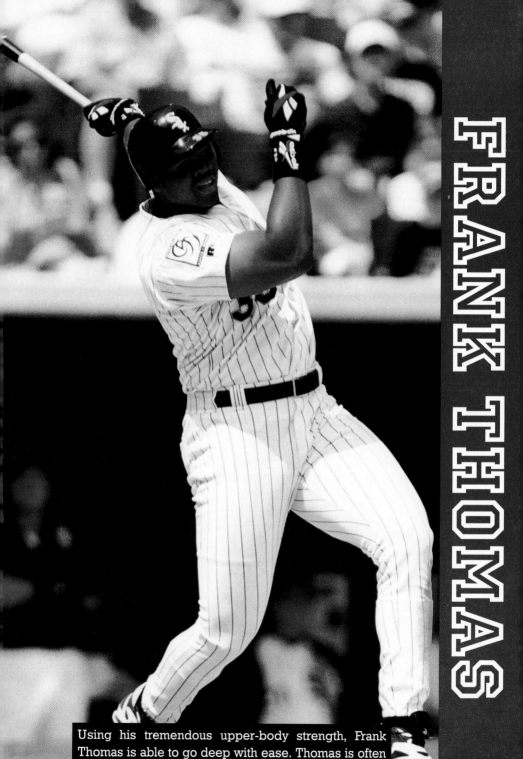

FRANK THOMAS

Using his tremendous upper-body strength, Frank Thomas is able to go deep with ease. Thomas is often among the league leaders in batting average, as well as home runs and runs batted in.

and proved he belonged. In 1991, his first full year in "The Show," he ripped 32 home runs, batted .318, and lead the league in walks and on-base percentage.

Two years later, he became the power-hitter everyone expected. Thomas—by then known as "The Big Hurt," for the pain he causes opposing teams and pitchers—blasted 41 homers and drove in 128 runs to lead the Sox to the divisional title. He was unanimously named the league's MVP. To prove it was not a fluke, Thomas slugged 38 homers in 1994, 40 in 1995, and 40 in 1996, even though two of those seasons were shortened by the players' strike.

The right-handed Thomas is a rare player, combining high batting averages with equally-high power totals, and walking twice as often as he strikes out. He uses an inside-out swing where his top hand is released from the bat during the follow-through. It is a style usually associated with slap-hitters, but it doesn't prevent Thomas from hitting the ball as far as anyone else in the game. In a home run-hitting contest prior to the 1995 All-Star Game, Thomas hit seven of the eight longest shots by any of the All-Stars.

At just twenty-eight, Frank Thomas should still have many productive seasons ahead of him. Barring injury, he is on pace to rank among the all-time greats by the time he is through. Entering the 1997 season, Thomas had career averages of .327 (batting), .456 (on-base), and .599 (slugging). Only Ted Williams and Babe Ruth exceed The Big Hurt in all three categories.

Confidence is the key to Thomas's success. "He has this ability that he thinks he's the best hitter," says teammate Robin Ventura. "He really believes it—and then he makes it happen."[1]

FRANK THOMAS

BORN: May 27, 1968, Columbus, Georgia.

HIGH SCHOOL: Columbus High School, Columbus, Georgia.

COLLEGE: Auburn University, Auburn, Alabama.

PRO: Chicago White Sox, 1990– .

HONORS: AL MVP, 1993, 1994; Major League Player of the Year, 1993.

When Frank Thomas first enrolled at Auburn University, he was mainly looked at as a football player. He switched to just baseball in his sophomore season. In 1989, he became the seventh player selected in baseball's free agent draft.

CHAPTER NOTES

Hank Aaron

1. Joseph Reichler, *Baseball's Greatest Moments* (New York: Bonanza Books, 1985), p. 235.

2. Bob Uecker and Mickey Herskowitz, *Catcher in the Wry* (New York: G. P. Putnam's Sons, 1982), p. 167.

Jimmie Foxx

1. Bob Broeg, "Awesome Sight—Mighty Foxx Swinging the Bat," *The Sporting News*, June 27, 1970, p. 19.

2. Joe Williams, "Rickey Was Cheap? Get a Load of C.M.," *New York World Telegram-Star*, February 28, 1956.

Harmon Killebrew

1. Mike Lamey, "Slugger Killebrew A.L. Player of Year," *The Sporting News*, October 25, 1969, p.3.

2. Dick Young, "Young Ideas," *New York Daily News*, January 17, 1975.

Mickey Mantle

1. Mickey Mantle interview with Bob Costas on *Costas Coast to Coast*, February 26, 1989.

2. Dan Daniel, "Mantle Makes Home Run History at 21," *The Sporting News*, April 29, 1953, p. 13.

3. Jim Ogle, "Mickey Mantle—Last of Yankee Super-Stars," *The Sporting News*, April 6, 1968, p. 8.

4. Ibid, p. 16.

Roger Maris

1. Associated Press, "Maris' Momentous Blast Wins Share of History," October 1, 1961.

2. Harold Kaese, "Maris Pegged Biggest Flop of '62 Season," *The Sporting News*, October 20, 1962, p. 14.

Willie McCovey

1. Lonnie Wheeler, "Willie McCovey: The Drive Hasn't Left Him," Gannett News Service Dispatch, April, 1980.

Fred McGriff

1. Deron Snyder, "MVP Just Wanted to Make Contact," *USA Today Baseball Weekly,* July 14–19, 1994, p. 35.

2. Bill Ballew, "The Crime Dog: Fred McGriff Sinks His Teeth into the National League," *Baseball Card News,* August 5, 1991, p. 14.

3. Ibid, p. 52.

Babe Ruth

1. F. C. Lane, "Can Babe Ruth Repeat?" *Baseball Magazine,* May 1921, p. 557.

Mike Schmidt

1. Bill Conlin, "Single Big Hit for MVP Schmidt," *Philadelphia Daily News,* October 22, 1980.

2. Bill Deane, "Schmidt Will Be the Sole Inductee in 1995," *Sports Collectors Digest,* November 25, 1994, p. 166.

Frank Thomas

1. Dave van Dyck, "'Big Hurt' is Worthy of Big Talk," *Chicago Sun-Times,* April 12, 1995.

INDEX

J
796.357
D

Deane, Bill
Top 10 baseball
home run hitters

J
796.357
D

Deane, Bill
Top 10 baseball
home run hitters

			17.95
MAY 0 8 2002	A.3533		
JUL 2 9 2002	1395		

6/00

Member of
Chautauqua - Cattaraugus
Library System